Beginners' Guide to Pattern Fitting and Alteration

Table of Contents

Introduction

I have a small fitting and alteration shop in New York and I am always swamped with work. From store opening to closing time, customers would come in and out. Weekends are particularly busy as the busy people of New York could only squeeze a free Saturday afternoon for an alteration. I even have standing orders three to six months in advance. Orders range from minor trouser length adjustments and fixing loose seams to major size readjustment and pattern modification. I don't think there will ever be a downtime for fitting and alterations as clothes are an essential part of our lives.

In my line of work, there are two moments in the alteration experience I enjoy the most. The first is hearing the reason for the customer's concern for alteration. I like talking with customers and how they relate with their clothes. When I was starting out, I would interact with them in a straightforward manner. I would simply ask them, "So, what do you want me to do?" and they would proceed to telling me how they want to add an extra pocket or trim the shirt edges. Customers were mostly in control, telling me what exactly they wanted me to do with their clothes. I was simply the alterations tailor: cutting and sewing according to my customer's specifications.

The more I grew in this business, the greater I felt I wanted to have a more active relationship with my customers. I began to have a regular set of customers and I felt bored with the routine of just executing commands. Instead of asking them what exactly they want me to do, I asked them, "With these clothes, what look do you want?" At first customers were startled with my question. They expected me just to be more technical and business-like. That opening would have them really thinking for some time but that question opened up a lot of conversations on people's thoughts on clothes and on how they want to look in general.

Some of the replies were quite interesting to hear.

"I want to look thinner."

"I want to make my hips look smaller."

"I want to emphasize my shoulders."

I took these replies and began customizing their clothes according to the look they want. This was such a refreshing change from the technical approach I was using with alterations. When I know what people want to look like, I can recommend certain alterations that will make my customers feel better about their clothes. It was also a teaching moment for me when I heard their projected look. For example, a client would like to make me trim her trousers just below the knee level. When I asked her what look she was aiming for, she said "I want to look taller." In principle, I agree that shortening the pants can make you look taller. But the length she wanted to go for will not really make her taller. In fact, it would even emphasize her short stature by exposing her entire leg. I recommended that we cut the trousers on the shin area, between the knee and the heel. We could even extend it only until above the heel. In this way, the illusion of long legs can be preserved. She had a look in mind, but her principles of design did not match that. It was a complete change for me, moving from a simple technical tailor to a proactive design collaborator.

There were other standout replies with my initial question. It was such a powerful question that people began opening up about their own lives. A simple question about clothes and looks could easily evolve into a conversation about how they feel about their body or the stress they feel from work. Some of the memorable answers were:

"I want to be able to wear my old clothes from ten years ago. These have a special memory for me, but I just can't fit into them with my current size."

"I want to look confident in my clothes. My bosses are critical of everything and I want to project an image of strength."

"I want to look beautiful. I feel I'm too fat and people around me are staring. I want to feel good about myself."

These anecdotes really touch my heart and make me realize how valuable my work is as a tailor. We may think that fitting and alteration is a simple cutting and trimming of clothes, but we are mistaken. When we are able to make clothes properly fit people, they feel better about themselves. When clothes emphasize the best part of people, customers feel a lot more confident about themselves. When trousers or dresses are able to hide unwanted contours, clients feel more secure about interacting with others. In our own way, fitting and alterations can make people feel beautiful and good about themselves.

I relish the second best moment in my alteration experience: the moment of fitting the new clothes. Usually, people pick up their altered clothes from the shop and try them on at homes. I encourage a lot of my customers to try it on in the shop and then we can make the necessary changes. This saves a lot of time especially when customers have extra alterations they want to make.I really look forward to seeing them look at the mirror in their newly-altered clothes. The smile on their faces and the confidence they exude as they parade their clothes around the shop is priceless. When alterations uplift people's moods and make them appreciate their own bodies, I feel that I have made a real difference.

This book is written to extend my humble fitting and alterations shop to your home. I really want to share that joy of making clothes work for people to everyone who appreciates and values these articles of clothing. I want to emphasize that everyone has that capacity to alter their own clothes. I have designed this book to be technically relevant to both beginners and those already familiar with the tailoring process. Each lesson is beautifully illustrated so that you will have a good visual that shows what I am talking about. Whether you are altering clothes as a hobby or for your established business, there is something new for you to learn in this book.

I want to make this book more interactive than other pattern-making books. I will describe general principles of design and the how-to for basic pattern fitting and alteration. I have designed each chapter as a mini-project for you to do. Don't just read this book as a leisurely, sit-down read. I envision that you have this book on your work table, and that you are reading the instructions as you are actually making your own clothes. With this book on the table and your hands on scissors and textile, we will accomplish projects and make the learnings really stick. The more clothes you work with, the more precise and accurate your alteration and fitting will be. Don't move too quickly through the projects until you have mastered each. This is not a race to finish the book in a day. Absorb what you can and then practice directly on real clothes. You will get better clothes after clothes, lesson after lesson.

These lessons are culled from my years of alterations and fittings. I will introduce you to basic patterns and fittings. I will also let you in on tricks and hacks I have learned along the way. Some people need to go to fashion school in order to sew and design well. I believe that any who is willing to take up tailoring seriously can learn from anywhere. With my guidance, you will be more confident in your pattern making and even in deciding how clothes fit people well.

I think that as long as people are growing, there is a need for alterations and fitting. People grow tall, get bigger, lose a few pounds, and develop more in some areas, all of which make them beautiful as they are. People develop in all sorts of proportions, which clothes manufacturers don't pay attention to. There are standard sizes like small, medium, large, XXXL: each person is different. The same person now will not be the same size or proportion ten, twenty years from now. Clothes don't grow with people. It is tempting to just buy new ones that fit your current size. A more practical approach is simply to alter your clothes to match your body size at the moment. With a good grasp of basic measuring, sewing and cutting, you will be able to continue using your clothes to fit you in whatever age or context you may be in. By altering and fitting clothes, you extend the lifetime of clothes and help people save money. When you begin to understand the beauty of design, you can transform old clothes into new ones, consequently transforming the person wearing them. Let this book be your guide, accompanying you to your journey as a great tailor and an instrument of transformation.

So what look do you want? Let the journey begin!

Chapter One:
Tools, Equipment and Accessories

I first bought my first set of sewing tools from a tool shop downtown. I remember starting with a tape measure, some scissors, thread and pins. My grandmother was very enthusiastic about my sewing so she gave me a box of colored thread I could use. To this day, I still keep that box with me, now filled with all sorts of pins, thimbles, buttons and a lot of good memories of my grandmother. From that initial set, I began to gather more materials as my shop grew. Each material I got had a memory and a story. Sewing materials grow with you through time.

All alterations must start with your basic tools. You must know the basic tools, equipment and accessories that are needed for you to be able to alter and fit clothes. Most of these materials are accessible and affordable. If you want to continue doing alterations for a long time or if you are thinking of turning your hobby into a full-fledged business, I recommend that you invest in quality materials. Some of my tools have been around for many, many years. If you switch too much between old and new tools, some alteration changes may occur. Hence, make sure that you have the right quality materials before you begin. There are five major categories of alteration tools: measuring, marking, cutting, sewing and accessories. I will be explaining the tools in each category. It may not be enough to just have one tool from each category as there are particular uses for each. Read through the descriptions and see if you will need these tools for your particular needs. For those who are planning to go professional, it is essential that you have all these tools at your disposal. Take in all the tools first before buying them. It is frustrating to keep on returning to the supply store if you don't have all your materials ready at hand. I will mark tools which I think are essential for beginners and those they can postpone until they have mastered the basics.

Measuring Tools

There are four tools which are needed to help you measure sizes. Each tool has a particular function that is more appropriate for particular situations. You need to have an accurate measurement both of the client and of the clothes to be altered. Problems arise when the measurement is off by even a few inches. Some tailors allow allowances in measurements to accommodate movement or possible changes in the client's body size. Make sure to note how to use each measuring tool.

Tape Measure

This is the most essential measuring tool you can have in your supply. Some tailors actually only use the tape measure for everything. But this is inaccurate. The tape measure serves a particular purpose, and that is to measure uneven surfaces. This is particularly indispensable when you are taking body measurements. The flexibility of the tape allows you to cover proportions accurately. You can also use the tape measure for patterns or textile when they are laid on uneven surfaces.

Most tape measures use the inch and metric systems. There are measures which place them both on the same side or on either side. This is good if you want to be as accurate as possible. You have to remember what measuring system you used: things can go awfully wrong when you measured in inches and recorded in centimeters. To avoid this error, use only one system of measurement as much as possible. Label all your measurements so that you don't get confused.

It is also worthwhile to compare the measuring systems. As I have said, try to stick with one system only. If there are cases when you need to switch, you have to know how the units are converted to each other.

Converting FROM	Is EQUAL to
1 inch	2.54 cm
0.4 inches	1 cm
1 feet	12 inches
1 yard	91.44 cm
0.01 yards	1 cm

1 inch	0.28 yards
36 inches	1 yard
1 mm	0.1 cm

When taking body measurements, there are fourteen measurements you need to obtain:

- neck

- bust

- waist

- hips

- front waist length

- back waist length

- arm

- shoulder

- knee

- calf

- instep

- side length to knee

- side length

- crotch

We will discuss how to take measurements for the different projects in the succeeding lessons. It is important for you to remember that the tape measure must accurately record these.

Measuring tapes can be made of fiberglass or cloth. There are those that come with an automatic recoiler and can be made to hold its position like a metal ruler. You need to take care of your measuring tape because they are very prone to damage. You will be using them on a number of surfaces repeatedly and the stretching process can distort tape and therefore the actual measurement. The material can also be frayed or damaged on the edges. Be careful also when you use the fiberglass tape. The edge can be quite sharp. I have a number of incidents when I released the hold dial on the fiberglass and it sliced my fingers. Practice with your measuring tape and observe safety always.

Yard/Meter Stick

When you have a piece of long fabric that needs to be marked, a meter stick is best to use. Usually, you lay the fabric on a flat surface and proceed to measuring using the meter stick. The rigidity of the stick helps you guide the main frame of the design and allows the cloth to be manipulated. You may even use the meter stick to smoothly drape the fabric on the flat surface. Do not use a meter stick for body measurements because it will miss out on the varying proportions of your clients.

Meter sticks can be made of wood or metal. Be sure to clean it properly and avoid dirt and soil from sticking. Place it somewhere cool so that the stick does not warp or fade. Let the tape measure ensure that the measurements are accurate and that you note what units of measure you are using.

Plastic Ruler

A handy measurement tool, the plastic ruler may suffice if you want to take small measurements within the fabric. They are helpful if you want to make minor adjustments during pattern alteration. It is especially useful if you have the transparent type so that you can also see the fabric as you take measurements. The pliability of the ruler allows for both straight and curve lines of short distances. Do not use this tool if you are taking body measurements or long fabric measurements.

Make sure to store plastic rulers in a cool environment. They are very prone to warping and thus increasing inaccuracy in measurement. Be careful not to let it come in contact with hot iron or chemicals because it may damage the ruler completely.

Seam Gauge

For those venturing into alterations as a profession, you may want to have a seam gauge. This tool is good for measuring short and repeated distances. What is good with the seam gauge is that it allows you to make marks on the fabric because it has a hole to accommodate a pin or a pencil. You may use this if for making patterns or knitting. It can even serve as a compass to make curves and circles pivoting on a center.

Hem Marker

When you are working with skirts, the hemline is important to measure. The hem marker is a measuring tool that rests on a firm base with an adjustable marker that runs vertically. This will let you determine how high you want your hemline to be in relation to the floor. If you are targeting a particular height, there are hem markers that can be pressed to release a powder-like chalk or talcum on the specific measurement. There are other models that have a clamp where you can put the skirt in and mark. You will want a hem marker to make sure that both sides of the skirt are symmetrical when draped properly. Problems arise when you just measure with a tape measure or a yard stick, but upon fitting, one side may lie lower than the other. The goal for skirts is also not to drag on the floor but also to achieve a certain distance from the ground according to the look your client may have.

Essential: Tape measure and yard stick

Nice to have: Plastic ruler, seam gauge and hem marker

Marking Tools

Marking becomes important when you begin transferring the pattern to the fabric. Patterns are your drawing board, the design you want the shirt, trouser or hem to look like. We will discuss more about pattern-making in another chapter, but it is enough that you understand how important they are in clothes construction. Like an engineer with a sketch of the proposed building, your pattern will reflect the final look of your clothes. It then becomes tricky to transfer that plan to an actual fabric. The goal here is to mark the fabric as accurately as the pattern sketch. The markings cannot be too conspicuous or fixed as they will be difficult to remove from the fabric. A good balance of easy transferability and erasable marking is thus targeted.

Dressmaker Tracing Paper

The most inexpensive material for transferring patterns is the tracing paper. The basic steps in marking follow a triple-deck sandwich manner: the pattern or tracing paper placed on a solid surface at the bottom, a thin barrier such as a plastic or tissue paper in between and the fabric on top. Your pattern can be drawn by hand or printed from pre-made sketches. You can use it directly but I recommend you still transfer it first to a tracing paper. Treat the pattern as a master template you can use for other designs. Therefore, to prevent it from being worn out, use a tracing paper instead when transferring to fabric. You can then mark the fabric following the pattern through a number of tools.

You must be able to see the pattern through the fabric. Otherwise, you will need to draw on the fabric. But most patterns are quite transparent allowing for easy transferability. When choosing a tracing paper, make sure that it is a lighter shade than the fabric so it retains the transparency. White is usually preferred as the standard.

When applying the markings on the fabric, be careful with the pressure you use. When you use pointed markers with great or sudden force, this can damage the tracing paper. Some tracing papers can be reused, but the thinness may really compromise the accuracy of the pattern. There are even some materials which can stain the fabric and then through the tracing paper. You have to note how the markings can damage your tracing so that you can avoid these.

Tracing Wheels

The tracing wheel then comes to create the markings on the fabric. This works best for making construction lines for seams or trims.

The way it creates the mark on the fabric is dependent on the model you have. Models are differentiated by the edges with which they make markings. Jagged or saw-toothed types of wheels create the lines by making hard and noticeable lines on the fabric. They can be quite rough on the fabric so be careful because they can damage it easily. Smooth-edged types create less visible markers on the fabric but do not damage the fabric. This is the ideal tracing wheel because it is inexpensive and preserves the integrity of the cloth. Needle-point types are the best and most professional tracing wheel-type available. They provide very subtle markings on the cloth and leave the least amount of damage on the fabric but these models can be quite expensive. It is up to you which model you want to start with; note how these different models can impact your fabric.

Marking Inks

The point of marking inks is for you to make a visible mark on the fabric based on the pattern. It is only used as a guide for you to know where to cut or sew so it must be erasable. You don't want a marking ink to be forever imprinted on the fabric. Hence, erasable marking inks are indispensable in doing alterations. There are a number of such erasable marking inks available on the market. Make sure that they are erasable for all kinds of fabrics. Test them first before you actually buy them.

There are two kinds of these products. The water-based ink creates a mark on the fabric that washes away with water. The ink washes away if you dab it with splotches of water. This ink is more manageable to use and creates even lines on the fabric; make sure that the fabric is not sensitive to water spotting.

The air-based ink can be traced on the fabric if you are a quick worker. This makes a mark on the fabric but disappears spontaneously within a day or two. If you dab it with water, it will disappear instantly. This is good if you are already familiar with the pattern and can do the work within one to two days. If you require more days or there are other alterations to be done on the fabric, the water-based ink may be more appropriate.

Chalk Markers

An alternative to inks are chalk markers. They also mark the fabric well and are easily erasable from the cloth but they can be quite tricky to handle. You would need the pointed chalk markers to outline the fabric well. Chalk markers can come in clay and wax form which are both easy to use. Clay markers also come in two varieties: brick and pencil type. The brick chalk marker comes with a pen-holder while the pencil is already shaped like a pen. Both options mark the fabric equally well. You will, however, need to constantly retrace the lines on the fabric as the brick and pencil markings become weak through repeated use. They are also very fragile so be careful not to drop them. They work in all types of fabric except wool, which will absorb the clay and leave a mark permanently. If you are going to use wool, the wax markers can be more appropriate. The wax marker will leave an oily spot on other fabrics which are not wool. The choice for which marker to use is dependent on the fabric that you will use.

Essential: Dressmaker tracing paper, choice of erasable ink or chalk markers

Nice to have: tracing wheel

Cutting Tools

Once you transfer the pattern into the fabric, you will need to cut the cloth accordingly. You might think that scissors are your only option. Actually, there are a number of cutting tools you can choose from which are more appropriate in certain occasions. Cutting is as crucial as measuring and transferring the pattern into fabric. It is not as simple as hacking away at a piece of cloth. There is an art to a smooth slice. It involves balancing the forces of the cloth being pulled in opposite directions as you cut through it. When cutting, there is a tendency for the cloth to move to a particular side and the measurements can be compromised. Therefore, you need a cutting tool that can slice through the cloth quickly without much resistance as to avoid any deviation from the intended cut.

When you are using a set of cutting tools, make sure that they are only used for that purpose. Do not use a pair of scissors that you are also using for other things such as paper, string, grass, etc. Using the blades on different materials will compromise its sharpness, and through time, will be too blunt to cut through any fabric smoothly. Dedicate your cutting tools only for clothes and store them in a safe place, away from children or near edges.

Most of these cutting tools are made of metal. Make sure that you don't keep them wet or else they will rust fast. Oil them once in a while to keep them working smoothly. Sharpen the edges so that they can cut through smoothly.

Scissors

Of course, you will need a pair of scissors as a basic cutting tool. Surprisingly, scissors are only used when you only need to make small cuts in a fabric. You use scissors to snip at threads when sewing or to correct small uneven lines. They are not used as the primary cutting material for large pieces of cloth. Do not attempt to use scissors with heavy fabrics because you will make the edges blunt while damaging the material unevenly. Like all your cutting tools, you have to keep your scissors sharp. Make sure that the handle fits your fingers well.

Shears

The primary cutting tool for all fabrics are your shears. They are bigger and heavier than your scissors and are therefore more suitable for cutting through large amounts of cloth. They are good with heavy fabric or multiple layers of clothes. You have to be comfortable handling shears well because they can be quite heavy to manipulate. When you feel that the shears are controlling your hand when you cut, then it is not a good fit. You should be in more control, so buy a pair of shears which you can best manipulate or will not cause excessive strain to your hands.

There are many kinds of shears depending on the shape of the edges. There are straight shears which are good for cutting through different types of fabrics at a smooth and fast pace. There are bent shears which are more curved and are appropriate if you really want to aim for accuracy in cutting. Then there are serrated or saw-toothed shears which are more appropriate for fabrics which easily move in place. The serrated edges keep the cloth in place and allows for a straighter cut. Again, choose the type of shears that will match the fabric you are going to work with.

Seam Ripper

You can use scissors if you want to cut through seams which you want to undo but a seam ripper will do the job faster and more efficiently. They can slice between threads and prevent you from damaging the fabric itself. The technique to unzipping stitches without cutting the fabric is to stretch the edges and cut through the stitches one at a time. Do not plod blindly and rip the stitches apart. This creates an uneven cut which will not look good. When one stitch is undone, simply pull the edges more and cut through with the seam ripper.

Essential: Scissors and Shears

Nice to have: Seam Ripper

Sewing Tools

Basic sewing tools are part of the essentials of any tailor. Whether you are more comfortable with hand-sewing or using a machine, you must be very confident in your sewing skills in order to make a good alteration. We will not be teaching sewing techniques in this book because that topic is better discussed in detail in another book. Basic sewing techniques can be learned easily. What you need to start out with are your basic thread and needles. These tools come in different sizes and colors which all depend on the fabric and the pattern you are using.

Thread

Threads come in many colors, materials, and weights and appropriate use must be observed. For example, the choice of the weight of the thread is equivalent to the weight of the fabric it is going to be used for. Delicate fabrics such as sheer and silk will need a light-weight thread. If you use heavier ones, the thread will stand out instead of blending with the fabric. For ordinary fabric, the medium-weight thread will suffice. For heavier cloth, use only the heavy-weight threads to hold the material together.

In terms of color, determine where the stitches will be placed. If you are going to sew a pocket, you can use any color for the inside pockets but if your stitch is somewhere noticeable, use the best approximation for the fabric you are using. Thread colors which clash with the fabric will stand out and that will not look good. The illusion you want to achieve is that the clothes are seamless.

In terms of material, there are a number of threads you can choose from. There are synthetic, cotton, silk and nylon among others. The general principle is of course to choose the material of the thread that closely resembles the fabric material. In general, cotton threads work with almost all fabrics so this will be a good investment.

Hand-sewing Needles

As with thread, needles come in different sizes. It is crucial for you to know basic hand sewing because a machine may bog them at times. So knowing what kind of hand-sewing needle is needed when you are beginning. There are stores which sell needles as a set already, lined according to sizes. The smallest are called your 'betweens' which you will use most of the time; because they are small, they allow for more accurate sewing. These needles may be difficult to manipulate if you have large fingers. The next size is called 'sharps.' They are longer and can be used if you are sewing through different layers or across greater distances. They are less accurate but they can accommodate more fabric. The biggest needles are called 'milliners' which also have large eyes. They are only good for basting long seams. Know which size is appropriate for the type of sewing you will be doing.

The thinness and thickness of needles also vary. The general principle is use thinner ones for lighter fabric and use thicker ones for heavy fabric. The goal of the needles is just to pierce through the fabric and hold the thread together. You must find that good balance so that your sewing can be uninterrupted.

Machine-sewing Needles

If you are really into alteration or making clothes in general, investing in a sewing machine can be a game-changer. It speeds up the work and allows you to manipulate fabrics in a more efficient way. There are several sewing machines in the market and you have to find one which you feel comfortable with. Choose a machine that is affordable and durable, that is perfect for your sitting height and will not cause undue strain, and that fits your working space well.

As with hand-sewing needles, machine needles also vary in sizes according to the fabric you are going to use. The principle also holds true that you use smaller or thinner needles for more delicate fabrics and for accurate stitching. Use thicker or longer needles for heavier or multiple fabrics.

Some tips on using the machine. Do not stitch over pins. I know this might be self-evident, but it happens a lot of times, especially when tailors forget to remove them. When the needle head hits the pin, the needle itself can be broken or chipped. If you do it repeatedly, the needle can be too blunt to sew properly so make sure that you remove the pins before stitching with the machine.

Pins and pin cushions

Another essential tool for any tailor are your pins.
When you want to fit the clothes on a client, you use a
pin to hold the fabric together at certain points. You
can use pins to mark areas for measurement or
cutting and to hold the fabric in place. Just be careful
that you don't stick the client when you are applying
the pin on the clothes. It is not a good experience to be
pricked by a pin accidentally.

Pins also come in varying sizes and thickness
according to your need. Follow the size principle of
shorter pins for thinner fabric, longer pins for thicker
or multiple fabrics. The type of pin will be more
important. Pins like those made from brass or nickel
do not rust easily, while stainless ones can corrode
occasionally. Do not use rusted ones anymore because
they may be a source of infection.

For safety, always place your active pins in a pin
cushion. Do not leave your pins lying all around. They
have plastic heads which easily roll and can disappear
in the carpet until somebody unfortunate enough
steps on them. Place the pins on the cushion all the
time when you are not using them.

Thimble

Not many people know how to use a thimble. As a
tailor, it is one of your best tools to prevent sewing
injury. Usually, accidents occur when you are
stitching very fast and the needle pricks your middle

finger. To prevent this, you place a thimble on this finger so you can avoid a painful accident and also prevent staining the fabric with blood. You want to make a good impression on your client so practice safety always.

Essentials: thread, hand-sewing needles, pins and pin cushions, thimble

Nice to have: sewing machine and needles

Accessories

Though not directly part of the sewing process, the measuring and fitting experience of your clients will need a few supplies. When a customer comes to you, your materials for measuring and fitting the clothes on them must be complete. Otherwise, you end up losing time as you look for tools when you need them at the moment. Have a kit on hand with you whenever you are entertaining a client. This assures you that you have everything on hand as the need arises.

Mirror

A full-body mirror is essential in any alteration shop or even at home. You need your client to be able to see his/herself fully. They need to see their anatomical body, their shape and contour, the proportions and the parts they want to highlight or hide. You also want them to see their back and their sides which they don't usually see. Some are very conscious of their figure so it is good to have them see themselves from all sides. Of course, you want them to see how the clothes look on them from all angles. You are selling your creation to them and the mirror is the best convincing agent you can use. When clients see for themselves that the clothes look good on them, they will return to you. If you hand over the altered clothes in a bag, there is not much connection between the two of you and there is a chance the client will need you to redo the alteration. Make the mirror your ally by allowing clients to see how good they look in your creation.

Notepad/Notebook

Take note of all measurements of your clients in one notebook. This is going to be your Bible of measurements so keep this very safe. When you have a notebook on hand, you don't forget the measurements at all. It is very frustrating for customers to be fitted with a tape measure over and over again because the tailor forgot the measurement. It is more disappointing to mess up your measurements because you forgot some crucial ones. You may have excellent memory but a notebook is more sharp than you are.

Plus, when you record measurements, you have a history of your clients. You will be able to record their growth over the years. You can say that they were size 28 ten years ago or a medium when they were younger. This helps you build rapport with them because you are able to remember all these tiny details about them. Loyalty is developed when customers feel that you really know them.

Corrugated Cardboard

When working with fabric, always have a flat surface. You want a steady base because your materials may slip and fall in all sorts of directions. Create a workstation in your room where you can place your materials safely. The cardboard can even have measurements on it for quick reference. You can use the board as a base to sketch patterns, drape fabrics, temporarily place pins, etc. The board also protects your table from damage. It is worth investing on a good corrugated cardboard because you will be using that on the table a lot.

These are the range of tools you will need when beginning to fit and alter clothes. I can never overemphasize the need to take care of your tools because they can last for a lifetime. Practice safety always so don't leave sharp objects just lying around. You don't need to buy expensive equipment if you are just starting out. Please do buy quality and durable materials because that can really affect the accuracy of your measurements and stitches. As a summary, I would like to recommend a list of essentials needed for your journey towards becoming a great alterations tailor:

1. Tape measure

2. Yard stick

3. Tracing paper

4. Erasable ink or chalk markers

5. Scissors

6. Shears

7. Thread

8. Hand-sewing needles

9. Thimble

10. Pins and pin cushions

11. Notepad

12. Corrugated cardboard

Chapter Summary

In this chapter, I have learned that:

- Alteration tools belong to five categories: measuring, marking, cutting, sewing, and accessories.

- It is worthwhile to invest on good quality materials.

- It is important to maintain the sewing materials in good condition as they affect the accuracy of measurements.

In the next chapter you will learn how to select patterns.

Chapter Two:
Selecting Patterns

Any alteration starts with a pattern. A pattern is simply a template of a dress, a skirt, a shirt or any piece of clothing that is transferred to the fabric to make clothes. There are many commercially-produced patterns available for males and females, for children and for adults. In determining the pattern to be used, there are two important questions you need to ask:

1. What is the body size and measurement of your client?

2. What are the patterns suitable for your client?

We will discuss these two crucial questions in this chapter. It is important for you to know that there must be a great harmony between your client's body measurements and the pattern you are going to choose. When your pattern does not fit your client, whether it is too small, too large, too tight or too loose, then your client becomes frustrated. You have to practice the art of matching the body size to the pattern. This will entail meeting a lot of clients and becoming familiar with a lot of available patterns.

First, you must have a good gauge of your client's body. Manufacturers will usually design patterns for an ideal figure from a statistical mean of all bodies studied. Remember, each client will be different.

When you evaluate your client's body, do not look at them as they should look like. Observe them for what they really are, and most of the time this deviates from the standard. You can accomplish this observation through the following methods:

- Mirror technique: Have the client face the mirror from the front, both sides and the back. Take time for each angle and notice every part of the body. It may be good to divide the body into 'heads.' Imagine that you are taking the size of the client's head and divide down, from the neck to the bust, to the waist, to the hips, etc. Note the natural posture of the client. While it is good for the client to always stand upright and tall, they usually don't in real life. The clothes may fit them well when they are standing tall, but will look loose or tight when they slouch in real life. Note all these changes and record them in your notebook.

- Photograph: Take pictures of the client from the front, both sides and the back. Ask for permission if you can store their picture for reference purposes. What is good with this technique is that you have at-hand access to the client's figure. In the mirror technique, you will have to rely on your memory of that measurement event and the objective tape measures. With a photograph, you can always refer back to the client whenever you want to confirm anything. Be careful that these photos remain private. Delete them as soon as the alteration is finished. Some clients will not agree to this because it may seem too intrusive, but explain to them the benefits of this method.

- Use a tape measure: The fool-proof method is really to take the client's measurements. We will discuss later on all the measurements you will need to take. This step is indispensable in every alteration project. This will serve as your objective guide in choosing the pattern and altering the clothes to fit your client. I highly suggest that you write all the measurements with the date taken and the units properly labeled. This will be your reference point for the client's measurements. They are specific to the date so you have to repeat the measurement at every point they come to you. Do not assume that they have the same measurements from last year or from ten years back. Measure them every time they come for an alteration.

I would recommend that you do all three techniques for every client visit. Some will object to having their photograph taken. At the very least, you must accomplish the mirror and tape measurement techniques.

Next, body sizes are different from males and females, children and adults. The same person will not have the same measurement as they age. It is good to know the standards for each age group and gender. Know that every client will differ from the standard, however minimally. The recommended sizes I will tell you will not always apply to your clients. Hence, customize it to how they really measure up, not just what their measurements should be.

There are three important measurements that will determine the pattern you are going to use: the height and build, the circumference, and the posture of the client. Each of these measurements provide a unique factor in determining which pattern to use. The height and build of the client will determine the pattern figure type. The circumference will determine the number size. Finally, the posture of the client will determine the pattern company you should be choosing from.

Height and Build

I will be discussing now the different standards of measurements for each gender and the age groups. When I say that the ideal height for a 36 year old male is 5 feet 10 inches, you know that this does not apply to everyone. I indicate the ideal to give you an idea of how pattern companies make their templates. In the end, the actual measurement of the client determines the pattern type you will use. You can have a 36 year old male whose height and build are more of a teen boy's type. You don't follow the age of the client; you follow their actual measurements.

When you measure the height and build, it may be good to measure the back as the reference. Start measuring from the most prominent upper vertebra, around the area they call as C7 or cervical bone 7. You can feel this as the spine bone that is most pointed and palpable at the level of the neck area, opposite the throat. Measure from this level to the level of the waist to get the height. For purposes of standardization, I will be using feet and inches to describe these measurements. Make sure that you are using the same measuring system or that you know the conversion to your preferred measuring system. You can go back to Chapter One to refer to the measuring tools for the conversion factors.

For Children

There are really no pattern distinctions between male and female children. The differences between the body types of the sexes are more apparent when puberty hits. Hence, this age group has one pattern for both sexes. They are all divided into toddlers and children.

Toddlers have a height of 28 to 40 inches. These are usually babies or those just beginning to walk. The shirt or dress is shorter than the entire length of the child. In terms of pants, the hips are larger and the crotch sizes are bigger to accommodate for a diaper.

Children pattern types are for those 35 to 48 inches long. The body length is of course bigger than the toddler size and the crotch depth is shorter because children will not usually require a diaper.

For Males

Body types are categorized according to boys, teens and men. The maximum pattern size is fitted for a height of 5 feet 10 inches. Individuals taller than that would still use the pattern for men with major alterations.

Boys' size types are good for those ranging from 48 to 58 inches. A basic bodice sloper is used for this age group. We will discuss slopers later on, but this basically means a dress template resembling the body. From the children's, the boy's size type has a wider shoulder for the shirt and a longer trouser length.

Teen Boys' size types are for those ranging from 5 feet 1 inch to 5 feet 8 inches tall. They are wider in shoulder length and longer in trouser length as compared to boys' sizes.

Men's size types are designed for those reaching 5 feet 10 inches. You will need to alter the pattern if your client is shorter or taller in height or bigger or smaller than the average size. You can make alterations for length and width from above and below the waist. The shoulders are quite similar to teen sizes.

For Females

Females have a wider range of sizes to accommodate the many bodily changes they have. For the height and build, we will not be incorporating the bust size yet, though it will affect these. The circumference measurements are most appropriate for the bust.

There are seven sizes for females according to body height and length. These are:

1. Girls's size type for those 50 to 61 inches tall.

2. Young Junior or Teen for those 5 feet 1 inch to 5 feet 3 inches tall.

3. Junior petite for those 5 feet 4 inches to 5 feet 5 inches tall.

The next sizes are for those with a more developed, mature body type. The height may overlap with the previous set, but the difference is in the body maturity.

1. Half size for those 5 feet 2 inches to 5 feet 3 inches.

2. Miss petite for those 5 feet 2 inches to 5 feet 4 inches.

3. Misses for those 5 feet 5 inches to 5 feet 6 inches.

4. Women: 5 feet 5 inches to 5 feet 6 inches.

For the half size, these are more for women who have narrower shoulders and short back waist length. The hips and the waist are also larger compared to the other types. We use the women's size type for those who have the height of the Misses, but have increased circumferences or build.

Circumference

There are two important measurements to determine the circumference of the person: the bust and the hips. Remember that these measurements are very particular in terms of age and gender. Bust and hip sizes change through the differently bodily developments as people change.

Bust

When you want to make dresses, blouses, coats, jackets or vests, the bust size is important. You measure it at the level of the elbow, rounding at the upper portion of each breast to consider the greatest circumference. Breasts may differ in size on the left and the right so just take the biggest measurement of the two. For women, you have to take the over bust, the bust and the under bust size, while for men, only one notation is used.

If the client has a cup A bra or a large bone structure, you can use a larger pattern size than recommended. Remember that it is easier to adjust the width or circumference of the clothes than the proportion at the shoulders and the arms. Having a larger size will accommodate the other body proportions and you can simply alter the width to make it smaller.

If the client has a bra cup size C or has a smaller bone structure, use a smaller pattern size than the recommended. This will fit better into the overall proportion of the person considering the shoulders and the arm length. You can simply adjust the width of the pattern.

Hips

When you want to make pants and skirts, the hips are important to measure. Look for the bony prominence on the side of the body below the belly button and that is the most likely location of the hips. From the hip measurement, you can adjust the pattern according to the size of the buttocks, the thighs, and the crotches. These are easily altered, but you have to get the hip measurement right.

Posture

The way a person is built and carries his or herself will determine which pattern company you will use. There are five established companies and they cater to a particular frame. When estimating the build of a person, have them stand tall first so you can assess the full height. Turn them to the side so you can see the width. Then, have them stand as they naturally do, without exerting effort. That effortless stance is the person's posture. Pattern companies specialize on particular frames in making their patterns.

McCall is a pattern company that specializes on average to tall figures, with a more prominent upper back than others. The bodice is longer and wider than all the other pattern companies. The bust tip is positioned ¼ to ½ inch higher and 5/6 inches farther from the center. This indicates a bustier figure.

In terms of sleeve caps, it is shorter and narrower than other patterns. Elbow circumference is also larger and the dart is transferred to the wrist level. This allows for a wider forearm circumference.

The skirt also has the widest width and the longest hem of all the patterns. The front waist dart is placed near the hip bones around a third the distance from the side to the center front. There is also more sloping from the hem to the waistline.

Butterick and Vogue cater to the average to tall figures. We take them as one category because their pattern sizes do not differ very much.

The bodice is shorter than McCall's by ¼ inch on the back. The shoulder and the width across the shoulder blades are the narrowest of the patterns.

The front neck width is curved less than McCall. The bust tip is placed lower than all of the patterns. The center length in the waist area is longer than

McCall's by 1/6 inches. The sleeve cap is placed higher and is wider than all of the patterns. The sleeve fits tighter than most to allow the elbow more room to move.

The skirt hips are smaller compared to McCall's. The side seam is not sloping and is almost straight. There are two darts for the front and another two darts at the back skirt which is unique to these two companies. The front darts divide the hips and waist in thirds. The back dart accommodates the upper hip and the buttock areas.

Simplicity designs for the average to shorter individuals. The back bodice length is shorter than Butterick and Vogue by 1/8 inches. The arm joints are slightly forwarded based on the back shoulder slope. The chest width is the narrowest of the patterns. The bust tip is at the same height as McCall. It has the same center length in the waist area like Butterick and Vogue.

The sleeve caps are shorter than Butterick and Vogue by ¼ inches, with the same elbow width as McCall. The basic dart is moved towards the wrist level to allow more width for the forearm.

Individuals with a smaller frame are more appropriate for Burda patterns. The upper back is slightly rounded and the arm joints are forwarded as evidenced by the dart size and the shoulder slope. The back bodice is shorter than Simplicity by 1/8 inches. The width of the lower bodice is narrower than the

American sizes. there is a shorter side seam and a bigger underarm dart. The bust tip is at the same level as Butterick and Vogue.

The sleeve circumference is the smallest of all the patterns. The elbow dart is also placed higher. The sleeve cap is designed for thin arms.

In terms of skirts, it is wider than Butterick and Vogue but not as wide as McCall. The side seam is slightly more sloped than Butterick and Vogue. The basic dart is placed near the hemline to allow more room for thigh and hip movement. The front and back width is the same as Simplicity.

Taken together, you must take note of the person's height and built, circumference and posture. All of these will determine the pattern you will use. Take the actual measurement of the client when you saw him or her, and not the measurements from before. The body undergoes many changes so the most reliable are the most recent measurements.

When you begin working with patterns, you will encounter two kinds: the sloper and the block patterns. The sloper pattern is more appropriate for your level. A sloper is often called the 'second skin' because it closely resembles the human body measurement. It is a pattern that is made from draping muslins on a model or dressform following body measurements. Since it uses the exact measurements, it does not allow for any movement if worn. It represents the most basic form of pattern which most home-sewers use. You will alter the sloper then according to the measurements of your client and the design you will incorporate.

You will be working with six kinds of slopers: the front and back bodice, the front and back skirt, the sleeves and the pants. From this base, slopers will come out the different dress forms if you now want to expand the outline. For example, the front and back bodices can be turned into your shirts, jackets, coats and blouses.

A block is a combination of slopers to produce the final pattern so you can combine a bodice and pant sloper to make a jumpsuit or a bodice and skirt to make a dress pattern. These are usually made by manufacturers. Blocks allow for different movements by creating seam and wearing ease allowances. They expand the sloper form into something more wearable. For your level, you can start with the slopers first and then try to combine them to form different blocks. The pattern construction is designed for particular people. You can edit pre-made slopers or you can even design and create customized slopers on your own.

For males, you can construct slopers into shirts, hood jackets, trousers and denim pants. You can create blocks from blazers by combining bodice and sleeve slopers. For females, you can create slopers into blouses, jackets and skirts. You can combine slopers into blocks by pairing bodice with skirts to make a party dress or a tunic. The basic dress forms can be expanded if you use different fabrics, different sizes and lengths, different accessories and pleatings. All of these will start with slopers and blocks.

Chapter Summary

In this chapter, I have learned that:

- To select a pattern, you must know the client's height and build, circumference and posture.

- Height and built are particular for different age groups and for men and women.

- There are five basic company patterns based on posture: McCall, Butterick and Vogue, Simplicity and Burda.

In the next chapter you will learn what fitting standards are.

Chapter Three: Fitting Standards

Have you ever seen ill-fitting clothes? What was your reaction? Of course, as an alterations tailor, people would come to us because they feel that their clothes don't fit them. We are so used to learning what should look good,we are trained to see what others don't. For example, if the skirt is too short or too tight, the person wearing it may feel restricted in terms of movement. It may draw unwanted attention and cause a scandal to conservatives. Or a baggy pair of trousers will always droop no matter how often you pull them up. A loose shirt may not always look fashionable and give the appearance of sloppiness. There is always a sense of wrongness visually when you see ill-fitting clothes on a person.

Of course, not everyone is gifted to be anatomically symmetrical. We may see models showing off their perfectly symmetric bodies in various fashion shows. They are more of the exception than the rule. All of us have some sort of imbalance, however minimal. As we age, even the most symmetrical body may develop some skewness. Some are leaning more towards the left, others are too busty or flat, hips may be drooping to one side. The clothes then follow these asymmetries and if not corrected, can highlight such differences. Since clothes are based on perfectly symmetrical bodies, they will not always look good as they are bought on ordinary people. If a skirt is drooping on one side, the other will compensate by lifting higher. With these variations in proportion, achieving harmony and balance becomes a challenge. When we know proper fitting principles, then clothes can transform asymmetric bodies into well-balanced forms.

Therefore, how clothes fit is important in any fashion designer or tailor. We want to create clothes that look good and fit well on people. This is achieved when we see a sense of harmony in the clothes. This means that all elements to the clothes contribute to the overall aesthetic beauty of the final look. One component of harmony is balance. We expect that when you wear anything, the right is balanced with the left, the front is balanced with the back. When we see a skirt from afar, we want to see that the right part of the skirt is hanging at the same level as the left. Otherwise, we say that the clothes don't fit the person. The balance is off and the harmony is disrupted, producing an overall bad look on the person.

Balance is achieved by two methods: the grainline and the structural line. These two contribute to the overall sense of balance in the clothes and how the clothes look on the person. The grainline focuses on the fabric, while the structural line integrates the clothes to the anatomic body.

First, the grainline refers to the alignment of elements in a fabric. Think of grainlines as imaginary horizontal and vertical lines lying perpendicular to each other in a fabric. This is easy to imagine in a fabric which is quilted or woven. We say that the garment has symmetric grainlines when elements of the clothes lie within these imaginary perpendicular lines. This can be challenging to imagine in fabrics that don't have explicit lines such as floral patterns or textured fabrics.

The grainline also is not just confined to the fabric itself, but also to the arrangement of fabric as a garment or a finished clothes. The designer can position the garment to be aligned to the grainline by manipulating the fabric so that its elements lie perpendicular to each other and the body. To help you remember the grainlines on a garment, mark vertical lines on the center front and back, the mid-front and mid-back, the sleeve capline and the seams on the side. They must all be parallel to each other. To mark the horizontal lines, place imaginary lines on the shoulder blade, the chest, the bust, the waist, the hips and the sleeve capline. All of these must be parallel to each other and to the ground. You have to train yourself in looking for the grainline in clothes to see if all the elements are aligned. If you still find it difficult to see the grainline just by looking, you can attach a weight on a string and place it on either side of the garment. The balance is achieved when both strings are hanging parallel to each other. From, here, you can appreciate the grainline.

Next, you can also achieve balance by observing the structural lines. This refers to how the elements in the clothes align with the anatomic body. We want to see clothes that mimic the symmetry (or the corrected symmetry) of a body. So like the grainline, we use the body references for vertical and horizontal lines (the center front and back and the hips for example). Next, we compare the different elements in clothes that should correspond as parallel to those imaginary perpendicular lines. We expect that the seams, darts, tucks, pleats and other elements of the clothes lie parallel either to the horizontal or vertical lines of the body. Otherwise, the garment will stick out or the body will look imbalanced.

When you construct clothes, you also have to consider the ease of the clothes. This refers to the lack of tension on the appearance of the clothes. There are two kinds: the wearing and design ease. The wearing ease refers to the degree of comfort the person wearing the clothes experience when moving with it. You want clothes where the person can be free to move forwards, backward, side to side without becoming stiff. Beautiful clothes which restrict movement may not be very sellable. We want to make the clothes as relaxing for the wearer that is why we have to create wearing ease on the clothes. This may mean allowing for extra fabrics on slopers. The second kind of ease refers to design. The designer can put various elements on a basic sloper such as pleats or pockets. These designs do not affect the movement of the person, but can contribute to the overall aesthetic merit of the garment. All of these elements must still conform to the overall balance of the clothes.

There are many elements that can be used to achieve this design ease. This includes: pockets, collars, darts, drapes, gathers, pleats and slits, and flares. We will discuss how each must be placed to achieve balance.

Pockets

Pockets can both be functional or decorative or a combination of both. They can be conspicuous or hidden. They can lie in the outward garment surface, inserted inside as a slash, or hidden in a seam. When you design pockets, they should be proportional to the overall garment and placed within the grainline and structural lines. When the pocket is placed in a body curve such as the hips, they should lie flat and smooth, not jutting out. The garment must also be designed to be loose enough so that the inside pockets do not become visible or that outer pocket openings remain closed.

Collars

Collars allow for a sense of depth in a garment. They hang around the neck and can be used to conceal scarfs or neckties. They are classified as flat, standing band, full roll or partial roll. The collar must be comfortable around the neck of the person, not causing undue strain. The outer edge of the collar must cover the back of the neckline and be placed smoothly on the garment. The ends should lie symmetrically. Lapels should be proportionate to the body. If you are going to change the garment neckline or the slope of the shoulders, the collar will also need to be changed accordingly. When one shoulder is slouching on one side, you can achieve balance by making the collar on the affected side smaller or shorter than the other.

Darts

You will see darts as the lines fabrics make when they are fitted on people, like fabric creases. Darts must give a feeling of lightness and symmetry. If you have one dart, it will enhance a body bulge. If you have two or more darts, they are placed parallel to the central bulge. This de-emphasizes areas where you don't want other people to see a bulge such as the stomach. Therefore, bigger body types will need more darts to create the illusion of smallness.

Gathers

Gathers are loose collections of fabric that hang on the edges of clothes to achieve a sense of lightness or fullness. Examples of gathers include bishop or puffed sleeves, a harem skirt or a blouson bodice. These tiny folds emanating from a single point gives an illusion of volume. For gathers that are controlled from the top, the edges should fall vertically parallel to the body line. For gathers that are controlled from the top and the bottom, there should be enough length as not to restrict movement.

Pleats

Pleats are usually long lines that extend from the top to the bottom of a garment created to add style to the garment such as umbrella or accordion pleats. The pleats must be controlled in such a way that they retain their shape even when the person is moving. When a pleat is placed on a bulge, you will need to create a lining. The garment must be tension-less even with such bold lines marking the garment.

Flares

A flare can be placed on the free edge of garments that creates the illusion of fullness or lightness. You can place flares in areas which are within the grainline especially on skirts and blouses. Because they divide the body into panels, flares must be symmetric and evenly-spaced. The flares you placed on one side must balance with the flares on the other side.

Chapter Summary

In this chapter, I have learned that:

- Clothes are assessed by how they follow the grainline and structure lines as the standard fitting patterns.

- There are garment fitting elements like pleats, gathers, tucks, vents, slits, darts, collars, drapes and pockets.

In the next chapter you will learn methods of pattern fitting.

Chapter Four:
Methods of Pattern Fitting

You picked out a pattern based on the client's height and built, circumference and posture. The next step is to fit the pattern to the specification of the person. Do not wait until you finish the garment before fitting it to the client. The most efficient way of proceeding with alteration is to customize the pattern first to the client before executing it on fabric. Make sure that you find a time to meet with your client to fit the pattern.

When you are fitting a client with patterns, utilize your full length mirror to analyze your client. Let them stand in a comfortable position, advising them to assume a good posture so that the final fit would be perfect. Provide a space where they can privately change. too cramped quarters may force them to assume positions they are not comfortable with. Advise them to wear snug-fitting underwear that they can comfortably display. Fitting involves some degree of intimacy with your client so make sure that they also feel comfortable to be in their underwear with your presence.

There are three methods of fitting patterns on your clients: pinned, trial garment and measurement methods. Choose the one that you feel most comfortable with. They are arranged here in the order most appropriate for beginners to experts. When starting out, it is good to use the pinned pattern. As you fit more clients, you will have a greater pattern and fitting sense so you can proceed with the other pattern fitting methods. Just make sure that you don't cause too much stress on your client with the fitting method you use.

Pinned Method

This pattern fitting method uses cutouts of your pattern and you literally fit them on the client. What is good with this method is that you don't use up the fabric itself before you actually need to cut it. This is the quickest fitting method to use so you don't delay the project. Since you are working just with paper patterns, you will need to exert more effort at imagining how the actual fabric will look like. But this method is best for figures who are easy to fit or if you are making loose garments.

As we have explained, slopers are the basic patterns you will encounter. When you are assembling the slopers into blocks or into a complete dress, it is good that you have a sense of how to place them. Do not make them too far apart from each other as when assembling the sleeves with the bodice. It will make the client bigger than they actually are. Do not place the patterns too close together because it will then give a false illusion of being too small. The proper method is really to overlap the patterns with allowances for movement. The overlap must just be right that will make the wearer comfortable when just standing and also moving about.

Before Fitting

I will now outline some basic steps on how to assemble the pattern before you meet a client. Do not assemble the patterns only when the client is there because it does take up a lot of time. I will also emphasize ways on how to strengthen your paper patterns so they do not become damaged during the fitting procedure.

1. Cut the individual pattern pieces with allowances. Do not cut too close to the edges since you still want to have the choice of adjusting the final pattern piece.

2. Reinforce your paper patterns. You can use either a cardboard, a sewing cutting board or a corkboard. This will prevent your pattern from becoming damaged from use. Simply place the pattern on the cardboard and cut around the edges. To make them stick to each other, you can use an aluminum foil in between the board and the paper pattern. Iron the three pieces so they adhere. You can even add a plastic wrap to cover all the pattern units.

3. When working with the crotch, neckline, arms and waistline, trim the excess patterns.

4. When placing the darts, make sure that the pin goes through and through the pattern to secure it.

5. Align the seam allowances by overlapping them along the stitching lines. To avoid any injury, make sure that the pins are placed horizontally or parallel to the stitching lines. Be careful about handling the patterns, remembering where the pins are placed.

6. Assemble all the pattern pieces together to remember how the garment will look like. It is important that you know how the patterns are related so that you can focus on the fit on the client. It is embarrassing to meet a client and you are still struggling where parts go together.

During Fitting

1. Prepare the client beforehand. Prompt them that you will be assembling the pieces on them to see the actual fit.

2. Start from the least complex to the most complex pattern pieces. Start with the skirt, then the vest, the bodice or the jacket and end with the sleeves.

3. To secure the pattern on the person, place a fitting band around the armpits or the armscye, the waist and the hips.

a. To do this, first, place the fitting band underneath or around the body part (armscye, waist or hips) and then secure with a pin.

b. Make two markings on the band. First on the endfold and the other on the exact spot where the fold is located. This is the center front.

c. Remove the band and fold them in between the two markings. Again, mark the midpoint this time as 'center back.'

d. Ensure that the markings are aligned. Use the bands to make sure that the pattern pieces don't fall off.

4. For skirts and trousers

a. Lift the skirt pattern piece to the waist line and the hips, making sure that the center front and back are aligned. Place the stitching line of the waist at the bottom of the band.

5. For the bodice

a. Place the bodice pattern in your model. Make sure that the arms go through the armscye first and then bring the pattern piece down the person. to test for movement, let the person place her hands on the hips or on the back of her head

6. Sleeves

   a. With the bodice piece already in place, slide
      the sleeve piece into the arms and fasten
      with the bands. Overlap the sleeve caps on
      the bodice and make sure that the arm can
      move freely. `

7. Make the necessary adjustment on the pattern
   pieces. If there are areas where you feel should
   be extended or cut, place markings on the
   target areas. If you want to remove areas on
   the pattern piece, you can simply fold it over so
   that you reach the desired length. If you want
   to increase the size of the pattern piece, you
   can insert extra pattern paper and fasten it
   with pins. Evaluate if all the hemlines are
   symmetrically in place. This is the part where
   you have to make all the necessary
   adjustments.

8. Make sure that everything is aligned. All
   vertical centers should align with the body
   centers. Dart lines should point to the fullest
   body bulge. Make sure that the client is
   comfortable with the pattern pieces in place
   both at rest and during movement.

9. Remove the pattern pieces and make sure that
   all the markings are intact. It is better to make
   the adjustments out of the model when the
   alterations are quite numerous.

10. Make the necessary changes on the pattern pieces. Utilize the pivot, seam or slash methods for areas where you pin or tuck-marked.

After Fitting

1. Make sure that all the markings are intact. Store them in a safe place until you will be transferring the pattern to fabric.

2. If the pattern has major revisions, it may be more useful to make a new pattern piece incorporating all the edits. Do not rely on the extra paper you pinned on the pieces while you were fitting if you want to increase the size. It is really better to have one solid piece of perfectly-matched pattern pieces rather than separate pieces.

Trial Garment Method

This method is ideal for those with atypical figures or variations from the standard. It may be too tedious or time-consuming for some, but how it fits the person will be more accurate in this method rather than the pinning method. This method is basically making an actual garment using an inexpensive fabric and trying it on the model. Usually, a muslin is used as the trial fabric to cut expenses and to manipulate the fabric quickly. If the texture is going to be a major issue, try to get the closest possible fabric with the same texture as the real one. When basting, you can choose to hand-sew or use a machine for quick sewing. Make sure that the trial garment is well-made and will not rip when fitted. This method will involve four stages: pattern preparation, fabric preparation, assembling the garment and fitting the garment.

Pattern Preparation

1. Cut all the pattern pieces you will need. Give generous allowances because you will still need to adjust. It is better to have more allowance than cutting the pattern too close to the actual.

2. On each pattern piece, indicate the lengthwise fitting at the center of the pattern.

    a. On the pants, half lengthwise at the level of the knee and extend through the whole pattern.

    b. On the bodices, indicate the center back and center front.

    c. On the sleeve, fold lengthwise at the level above the elbow and extend.

3. On each pattern piece, indicate the crosswise fitting at the center of the pattern. Mark the lines along the sleeve capline, chest, shoulder blades, and hips as they are all parallel to the hemline at the ground.

Fabric Preparation

1. Assess the grainline of the fabric. Make sure that the lines of the fabric are lying perpendicular to each other.

2. Place the pattern pieces corresponding to the grainline of the fabric. Mark pins to keep the pieces in place. Reinforce the pattern along the pattern pieces with more pins.

3. Add more pins around 2 inches away from the pattern pieces in the fabric itself. The fabric will move when you begin to cut it so it is good to have reinforcements both inside and beyond the pattern pieces.

4. Begin cutting the fabric along the pattern pieces. Make allowances for alteration.

5. Transfer the center front and back, the crosswise and lengthwise markings from the pattern to the fabric using a pencil. These will be important for assembly.

Constructing the garment

1. Place the pieces on a flat surface. Overlap them at the stitching lines to see the complete garment assembled.

2. You can baste the patterns through a number of ways.

a. Pin-basting: From one end, fold the fabric along a dartline. Lay the fold symmetrically on the other and secure with a pin. Make the seam lines of the separate pieces meet and secure with a pin.

b. Hand-basting: Do the pin-basting first as noted above. Then, do slip-basting along the folded edges.

c. Machine-basting: Make sure that you are stitching the seam allowances and the darts inside the garment. Start with the longest stitch and sew without creating tension on the garment.

Fitting the garment

1. Start fitting the pieces separately starting from the easiest to the most complex. Start with the skirt, then the bodice, then the sleeves last.

2. Make the necessary adjustment on the garment as it is fitted on the model. If it is too tight, loosen some of the stitches and re-stitch. If the garment is too loose, pin tuck the garment and then stitch until the desired length is achieved.

3. Ensure that fitting standards are in place.

4. If all the adjustments have been made, stitch the trial garment as a single garment. Be aware of the hem as it should be symmetrical. Try it

on the model again and create the final adjustments.

Measurement Method

This method is the most convenient for clients because they do not have to change clothes or have patterns or garments attached to them. All you need to do in this method is to take their bodily measurements. This is quite tricky because you have to complete all measurements on the client because you don't have the benefit of a trial garment or a pinned pattern. You will be transferring the measurements on actual fabric so the leeway for error is smaller compared to the other methods. I recommend this method if you have been measuring a lot of people and that you are confident that you are accurate in your measurements. We will be discussing all the measurements on the different body segments for each pattern piece.

Lower Body (for making skirts and trousers)

1. Centers: measure from the waist at the bellybutton level to the floor.

2. Inseam: measure from the crotch to the floor.

3. Knee position: measure from the middle of the kneecap to the floor.

4. Side seam: measure from above the hips to the floor.

5. Hip depth: measure from the waist to the hip joint at the center front, back, and both sides.

6. Crotch length: measure from the center waistline front to the center waistline back passing through the crotch.

7. Waist circumference: measure from center back to the both sides. Measure center front waist to both sides. Record the two measurements.

8. Hip circumference: measure from center back hips to both sides. Measure center hip front to both sides. Record the two measurements. Take into account the size of the buttocks.

9. Thigh circumference: measure the fullest length of the thigh above the knees. Measure that from the waist.

10. Additional measurement. Though not required, these measurements can be taken for completeness.

    a. Knee circumference: measure the fullest knee length when the person is sitting or squatting.

    b. Calf circumference: measure the fullest part of the leg below the knee.

c. Heel-instep circumference: measure the foot from heel on one side to the heel on the other.

Upper Body (for the bodice)

1. Body centers: from the back, measure the bony prominence at the back at the highest level on the level of the neck to the lower edge of the waistline

2. Full bodice length: measure the back, from the shoulder to the waist. Measure the front from the bust to the waist.

3. Full bodice width: from the center back, measure to both scye level sides. From the center front, measure length to both scye level sides. Record the two measurements.

4. Side seam length: Measure from ¾ to 1 inch below the elbow to the waistline

5. Shoulder width: Measure the shoulder from tip to tip, passing through the scyeline in front and at the back.

6. Shoulder slope: `Measure from the center back waistline to the shoulder tip of each side passing through the shoulder blades diagonally. Repeat for the front. Record the 4 measurements.

7. Shoulder length: measure side neck out to the shoulder tip of each side.

8. Chest length and bust contour: starting from the mid-shoulder, measure the contour of the breast until you reach the rib cage on the under edge of the bust.

9. Width of shoulder blade. From the back, at the level of 1 to 1 ¼ inches above the elbow, mark the arm crease. Measure the length from one arm crease to the other side passing through the shoulder blade. Repeat at the front.

10. Blade and bust tips: measure from the edge of one shoulder blade to the next and from the tip of one bust to the next.

11. Bust and shoulder blade length. Measure from the edges of one shoulder blade to the waistline and record the other shoulder blade to the waist line. Measure the bus tip of both sides to the waistline.

Arms (for the sleeves)

1. Underarm length: Measure from the level of ¾ to 1 inch below the elbow to the wrist line.

2. Elbow tip position: Measure from elbow tip to the wrist line.

3. Overarm length: Measure from the shoulders to the elbow to the wrist line.

4. Biceps circumference: Measure the fullest part of the upper arms.

5. Elbow circumference: Bend the elbow at 90 degrees. Measure from the elbow tip across the crease to the elbow tip again to complete 360 degrees.

6. Wrist circumference: Place 2 finger on the wrist line and measure the circumference at that level.

7. Hand circumference: position the thumb to level with the index finger. Measure the circumference of the hand as it passes through the base of the thumb.

Chapter Summary

In this chapter, I have learned that:

- There are three fitting pattern methods: pinned, trial garment and measurement methods.

In the next chapter you will learn methods of pattern alteration.

Chapter Five:
Methods of Pattern Alteration

There is an art involved in pattern alteration. It involves the customization of the pattern chosen to the specific measurement of the person. From the fitting, you must be able to note all the necessary adjustments either from the pinned, trial garment or the measurement methods. It is not good if the garment you produce will still have a lot of major adjustments once you work on the fabric. Study the measurements of your client and evaluate where they are exactly placed in the pattern pieces. I will be showing you a general procedure for alteration and then the different methods of alteration.

How to Alter

1. Take a look at the big picture. Look at all the adjustments you have to make and how they relate within one pattern piece and with each other.

2. Choose a pattern alteration process that is appropriate. There are three methods you can choose from: slash, seam and pivot.

3. Place the pattern and work on a flat surface, whether it is a board or a reinforced surface. Iron out paper or fabric so there are no creases.

4. Proceed systematically when addressing adjustments.

   a. Start with the length. Make adjustments, either increasing or decreasing the length of a piece.

   b. Follow with the width. Make adjustments, whether shortening or widening the width of a piece.

5. Ensure the accuracy of all the adjustments. The final garment must not produce any tension like unnecessary creases, but should look flowing and flat.

Seam Method

The seam method is the safest for beginners. You will now be cutting through the pattern pieces but you will only be manipulating the edges or the seam allowances. You will be cutting the seam allowances from the concerned edge and never the interior of the pattern. The adjustments are quite easy and simple to do. Be careful that the seam allowances you made are clearly marked because they don't maintain their forms in this method. Here are the methods of seam alteration:

1. Locate the concerned stitching line for adjustment.

2. Locate the pivot points on the stitching line. These are areas where there is greatest

variation or where uneven and even changes are present.

3. Create clip lines from the edges cutting across the seam allowances to reach the pivot points.

4. Place the alteration paper underneath.

5. Cut the concerned seam allowance.

6. Create hinges to allow movement of the pieces by cutting through the clip lines

7. Make sure that the pattern area is secured to the alteration paper

8. Appropriately change the loose pattern pieces according to the degree needed.

    a. Slide the seam away from the pattern area to increase an even amount of length or width needed

    b. Slide the seam towards the pattern area to decrease an even amount needed

    c. Pivot the seam away from the pattern to increase an uneven amount needed.

    d. Pivot the seam towards the pattern to decrease an uneven amount needed.

    e. If there are even and uneven changes, make the necessary even changes first before the uneven ones. Slide then pivot.

9. Secure the changes to the alteration paper.

Slash Method

When you say slash, you are really cutting through the pattern from the side to the interior. This method involves adjusting the pattern by cutting through the interior of the pattern of the concerned body area, either to increase or decrease the size. This is good if the pattern really needs to be adjusted evenly on one side. This method is quite challenging if you have multiple points of adjustments which are not even. It can be prone to distortion as the biggest adjustment length can overpower minor but important size adjustments. Here are the procedures to accomplish the slash method:

1. Plan adjustments near the edge of the change you want to correct.

2. Create a method for evaluating all the necessary changes in the pattern piece.

   a. If the change is even, you can proceed to extending the line across the pattern

   b. If only one seam line is to be changed, mark the alteration line as it crosses the concerned seam and continue as a straight line. Make another line between the alteration line and the line cutting across the unaffected seam.

c. If only the interior needs to be changed but not the seamline, mark a line extending from one stitching line to another in the same affected area.

d. When you have both even and uneven changes, mark the line from the pattern edge of the concerned area and extend. These lines should note when the changes from even to uneven.

3. Form hinges on the stitching lines by putting clips on the seam allowances. This will allow for movement in the parts of the pattern and maintaining its flatness.

4. Place the alteration paper that will mark the area.

5. Cut the alteration paper along the slash lines.

6. Pin and combine the areas you have altered to the unchanged areas in the pattern.

7. Appropriately change the loose pattern pieces according to the degree needed.

a. Separate the patterns in the same amount parallel to the increase of even length or width needed

b. Overlap the patterns in the same amount parallel to the decrease of even length or width needed

c. Pivot the pattern edge away from the interior of the pattern to increase an uneven amount needed.

d. Pivot the pattern edge towards the interior of the pattern to decrease an uneven amount needed

e. If there are even and uneven changes, make the necessary even changes first before the uneven ones.

8. Pin and secure the final manipulated pattern areas to the alteration paper.

Pivot Method

The pivot method attacks the alteration problem differently from the others. The previous patterns would need to cut from the pattern piece itself, whether the interior or the seam allowances. With the pivot method, only the contour edge of the pattern is altered. You start with making a copy of the area where you want to alter, whether to increase or decrease in size, whether evenly or unevenly. You take this duplicate and place or pivot it on the existing pattern and then retrace the whole pattern, incorporating the alteration. In this way, you don't disturb the grainlines. With this method, you can incorporate a lot of variations of alterations and still come up with a cohesive final pattern. Be careful at marking the new cutting lines because they can be obscured in the final tracing. To avoid this, use a bright ink like red to trace the final outline. Here is the complete process of the pivot method:

1. Indicate the areas in the stitching line that needs to be altered. This could be areas where there are a lot of even, uneven or a combination of both, alterations are located. There could be more than one pivot point in a given area.

2. Use another pattern paper and trace the outline of the pattern area of concern.

3. Create a new pattern edge on the edited pattern.

4. Pivot the duplicate on the original pattern according to the degree of alteration needed:

   a. Pivot the duplicate beyond the original to increase even sizes.

   b. Pivot the duplicate inwards to the original to decrease even size.

   c. Pivot the duplicate away from the original along the stitching lines to increase uneven sizes.

   d. Pivot the duplicate towards the original along the stitching lines to decrease uneven sizes.

   e. If there are even and uneven changes, make the necessary even changes first before the uneven ones.

5. Secure the properly positioned duplicates on the original. Make sure they don't move during the tracing.

6. Trace the new outline of the pattern piece. Mark the new outline with a bright marker like red.

7. Cut the new pattern pieces and mark the new stitching lines.

These three methods are the most common ways you can alter the new pattern. Familiarize yourself with all three because there are some changes that are more appropriate for each method. For example, if there is a greater area of even change you need, a slash method may be more efficient rather than retracing the whole outline using a pivot method. If there are only small changes involved, the seam method will be more helpful. If you have a lot of variations with both even and uneven characters, the pivot method will be more useful. Regardless of method, make sure that the edited pattern is free of tension and maintains the grainline.

Chapter Summary

In this chapter, I have learned that:

- There are three methods of pattern alteration: seam, pivot and slash methods.

- It is important to know which technique is to be used for symmetric and asymmetric changes.

Chapter Six:
Project I: Hands - Alter the Sleeves

Are you ready to begin your alteration projects? I'm sure that with all that you have read so far, you are excited to apply the lessons to actual patterns and fabrics. I have written seven simple alteration projects which you can try. These are the most common problems you will encounter when you begin alterations and so we will start you off with the most basic ones. I have designed each project to tackle a particular fitting problem that you will most likely encounter when you begin receiving clients. I suggest that you do not rush through these projects, aiming for perfection before you proceed. These projects are meant to be enjoyed so take as much time as you need.

The chapters are designed into a structure that will allow you to proceed in a systematic pattern. You begin with analysing the body of your client first and identifying what is inherently problematic with the structure. Next, I will discuss typical fitting errors you will encounter in reference to the body size of your client. Next, we will take the fabric and highlight what needs to be done to address your client's problem. Then we will proceed to a step-by-step process of alteration. Through this method, you will be able to move more efficiently and commit less errors.

We begin with basic bodice patterns. Jackets and sweaters are the typical Christmas gifts of aunts and mothers to teenagers. You will always get a hand-knitted sweater with the most festive colours. The fit on the shoulder and the overall design may be quite charming. Often, it is the sleeves which make all the variations. I have encountered clients with sleeves hanging out from their hands like scarecrows. The usual remedy is to pull the extra sleeves back so it becomes bundled over the arm or the forearm. It can restrict movement and can be aesthetically unattractive. But altering sleeves are one of the easiest projects you can start with.

Analyse the Body

When you encounter arm sleeve alterations, it is good to analyse the entire arm from the tip of the shoulder to the elbow to the wrist line. The growth of the arms is not even for everyone, so we can detect variations of length before or after the elbow crease. In people with shorter arms, the bones of the arms or the forearms may be shorter than average. There are also cases where the hinge flesh which anchors the arm to the torso is formed closer to the rib cage making the entire arm shorter. You have to decide which part of the entire arm is shorter, if it is the arm above or below the elbow. This is where you make the necessary adjustments.

Analyse the Fit

The dart of the sleeve must align with the elbow joint. If the dart lies higher than the elbow joint, the forearm area may be too restricted in its movement because of the tight fabric. But if the dart lies below the elbow, there is more room in the arms which gives an illusion of puffiness or a big volume.

The sleeve hemline must also be exactly at the wrist line. If it is above that line, then the sleeve is too short. If the hemline is beyond the wris tine, it can hide the hand and make it look stubby. So you have to monitor both the elbow joint and wrist level and adjust which part of the arm is most concerned.

Fabric Needs

If the upper arm is bigger than average, then more length is needed above the elbow joint. If the upper arm is smaller than average, less length is needed. This also goes for the forearm in terms of distance from the average. You have to adjust which part that will make the dart coincide with the elbow joint and the sleeve hemline to coincide with the wrist line.

Recommended Alteration Method

1. First, measure the arm circumference and length of the client, as well as the elbow and wrist circumference. Do this for both arms

because not all arms measure equally on both sides.

2. Based on these measurements, decide what part of your client's body does not conform to typical fitting standards. It may be that the client has a shorter arm than the forearm. Once you have decided which part of the arm needs to be adjusted, mark the area on the fabric where you want the elbow and wrist line to be.

3. Using the slash method, you can adjust the concerned portion. Cut the pattern according to the adjustments needed. When you are satisfied with the pattern, you can translate it to the fabric.

4. In the case of short arms, you can cut the length of the fabric so that the dart is at the elbow joint and the hemline is at the wrist line.

5. Start cutting the fabric according to the adjustments in the pattern. Give some allowances and then stitch the sleeves.

6. Press the hem of both sides to flatten the sleeves area.

7. Fit the clothes on your client and see if there are minor changes to made.

Chapter Seven:
Project II: Neck - Widen the Front Neckline

There are some shirts or jackets which can choke a wearer because the neckline is too tight. And there are some women who want a bigger neckline to expose flattering neck angles. Whatever it is, the neck can be quite tricky to alter. You have to measure the neck circumference and indicate the areas you want to expose. You have to be careful that the new neckline will allow the wearer to be comfortable but also modest-looking.

Analyse the Body

Try to understand the cause for the discomfort. There are people who have larger neck circumferences than the average person, whether it is because of more tissue deposits in the area or more developed muscles.

Analyse the Fit

When you have a neckline that is too tight, the back neckline rises. There is also a circular wrinkle forming below the front neckline indicating tension in the fabric. The front armscyes may also look larger as the fabric is pulled down. The shoulder blades and chest fitting lines also rise because of the tension upwards.

Fabric Needs

When you have a client who has a larger than average neck circumference, the neck opening must be wide at the sides and low at the center front. In this way, the fabric will relax and the shoulder blades and chest fitting lines will return to their normal position.

Recommended Alteration Method: Slash Method

The goal is to widen the back and front neckline while lowering the front neckline. You can adopt the slash method for this.

1. Measure the client's shoulders, neck circumference and chest width. This will give you an idea how large the neckline needs to be. Make sure that the client can move freely with the new neckline while not exposing intimate parts of the client's body.

2. Create a fitting garment with the appropriate pattern according to your client's measurements.

3. In the fitting garment, cut through the neckline seam allowance at ½ inch intervals in the center front area as needed to widen the neckline.

4. Check if this will relieve the tension on the bodice. Continue cutting until there are no more creases seen.

5. Mark the area where the tension is relieved and then extend the cut sideways until you cover the entire front neckline.

6. Proceed in the same manner with the back neckline cutting close to the shoulder seam.

7. Draw the new neckline using the front and back necklines. Stitch all seams.

8. Iron the neckline and the entire bodice to flatten the clothes.

9. Let the client try the clothes on and adjust any minor changes needed.

Chapter Eight: Project III: Waist: Change the Seam

There are shirts and dresses which fit well on the shoulders and neckline but look voluminous in the waist area. For bustier models, the overhanging fabric may make them look bigger than they really are. When you have too much fabric in the waist area, the bodice may even extend to the hips and thigh areas. The overall look is unattractive and this would require altering the very waistline of the fabric.

Analyse the Body

Understand what part of the body is not proportional. There are some models who have tighter abdomens and hence, their stomach is jutting out less than the average person. Posture also plays a role. If the person is standing overly erect, almost extending the back, the waistline usually will become smaller. In hourglass types of figures, the waist is considerably thinner than the ribcage and the hips. Their sides are also more sloped and longer from the arm joints to the waist.

Analyse the Fit

The fabric usually crumples or is baggy at the waist area. Vertical folds appear as the extra fabric bunches.

Fabric Needs

You will need to either take out the excess cloth or convert it to details such as pleats or drapes or any stylish detailing. I would recommend decreasing the length of the waist area and let the garment flow more closely to the body contour.

Recommended Alteration Method: Slash Method

The goal is to narrow the side area of the waist. You can accomplish this through the slash method.

1. Measure the client's waist area from the centre back to the sides and the center front to both sides.
2. With the client's measurements, select the best fit pattern and create a fitting garment. Take the fitting garments and place it on a flat surface.
3. Create tucks of equal width on the waistline, both in front and at the back, near the side seams.
4. Distribute the tucks evenly and then cut the excess. Adjust until there is no more tension in the fabric.
5. Taper the tucks towards the armscye seam line. Stitch all seams.
6. Iron the clothes to flatten it.
7. Let the client try the clothes on and adjust any minor changes needed.

If you are going to be altering a skirt, pants or trousers to fit the new waistline, you will follow a similar technique. Still use the slash method:

1. Take the appropriate measurements on the client (waist, hip, leg length, crotch area, hemline).

2. Select an appropriate pattern for the client's measurements. Create a fitting garment based on the pattern.

3. On the fitting garment, release the waistline seam on each side of the seam area.

4. Form tucks on the front and back near the seams until the excess fabric is removed.

5. Make sure that the new pants retain a wearing ease that will still be comfortable to the client.

6. Taper the tucks to the side seams until the tucks disappear. Stitch all the seams.

7. Iron the skirt or the trousers to flatten the clothes. Examine if the new fit is within the structural lines.

8. Let the client try the clothes on and adjust any minor changes needed.

Chapter 9:
Project IV: Chest Alteration - Loose Fitting Garment

There are garments that don't look flattering on the chest area. When you pick out a garment that is too big on you on the chest area, the extra fabric will make you disproportionately more voluminous on the thorax. There are many reasons for this including a smaller upper back, a smaller chest or a flatter bust size. To alter the chest area, you will need to measure all the pertinent bodice or upper trunk measurements we have outlined in Chapter Four.

Analyse the Body

Notice the different parts of the upper trunk. The rib cage may be smaller than average. The upper back or chest muscles may be less developed. The person may also be standing too erect so that the back is flat, which can decrease its size or transfer the fabric to the shoulder area. The distance between the arm joints may also decrease.

Analyse the Fit

When fabric is too loose, the extra fabric hangs loose in the chest, shoulder blade or armpit area. If you raise the arms forward, the armscyes will cut against the arm hinges. If you lift the hands upward, there is less movement as the sleeves are pulled against the arm.

Fabric Needs

You will need to decrease the fabric at either the chest area or the shoulder blades. The change will also affect the scyeline and the armscyes. This will lessen the tension in the area and allow more fluidity in movement.

Recommended Alteration Method: Slash Method

The goal is to cut the excess fabric at the chest and shoulder blade areas. The slash method is recommended for this.

1. Make the necessary measurements on the client (chest width, bust size, bodice length, shoulders, waist).

2. Choose a pattern that fits your client's measurements. Create a fitting garment according to the pattern. Make the necessary adjustments on the fitting garment before you translate it to the fabric.

3. To tighten the chest area, begin by forming a vertical tuck around 1 inch from each armscye.

4. Remove the excess fabric in the chest area until the tension is relieved.

5. Adjust the widths on the fabric until it becomes smooth.

6. Taper the tucks near the shoulder and the scyeline. Stitch all the seams.

7. Iron the entire bodice to flatten out the clothes. Make sure that the new fit is within the structural lines.

8. Let the client try the clothes on and adjust any minor changes needed.

Chapter 10:
Project V: Broad Hips - Loosen the Pants

I have a number of clients who come in for alterations because their pants don't fit anymore. This may rather be embarrassing because some of them have really grown, especially in the hip area. They say that they are usually a size 26 but they can't pull up the pants completely to the hips. Or they will try to force the pants through but there is much restriction in movement that they open the buttons to let their waist breathe a little. This rather common problem has a simple solution that can end your clients' embarrassment. It may need a lot of acceptance of their current form but it is possible to still wear your old pants.

Analyse the Body

Measure the hip area again from center back to the sides and the center front to the sides. Compare this with the standard hip size for the persons built and height. People with bigger hips either have a bigger bone structure, or more deposits of soft tissue in the joint area.

Analyse the Fit

When you fit their old pants or a pair of pants they want to fit in, there are creases and tension on the hip area. The rest of the trousers will be pulled up as a result, so watch out for the hemline. Sometimes, the pants cannot actually come all the way up to the hips because it is stuck in the crotch area.

Fabric Needs

You will need to adjust both the width and the length of the pants especially at the hip area. this will also create longer side seams curved near the hipline. When you have more fabric in the hips, the rest of the trousers can extend to the intended length.

Recommended Alteration Method: Pivot Method

1. Make the necessary measurements on the client (waist, hips, leg length, crotch).
2. Choose an appropriate pattern based on the measurements.
3. Calculate for the amount of fabric you will need. This is obtained by measuring the garment you are going to alter and subtracting the sum of the total body hip measurement plus the wearing ease.
4. Now, divide this difference into four to compute for the side seam allowances.

5. Trace the new side seam measurement on the hipline area. Curve back near the original seam line and below the thigh area.
6. If you feel that the legs have also become wider, extend the new line parallel from the original starting point from the hipline to the end of the hem. This adjusts the legs to match the adjustment on the hips. Stitch all seams.
7. Iron the trousers to flatten the clothes. Observe if the new fit is within the structural lines.
8. Let the client try the clothes on and adjust any minor changes needed.

Chapter 11:
Project VI: Short Legs - Trim the Garment

You might like a particular fabric of pants but your legs are too short for the actual length. The usual solution is of course to have the pants altered by a tailor to your desired length. You can do this for yourself or for others if you understand leg measurements and how to trim garments properly. This is one of the easiest projects you can undertake because the process is quite straightforward.

Analyse the Body

The legs of your client may be shorter than average, whether it is shorter above or below the knee. Compare the client's leg measurements to the standard for their height and build.

Analyse the Fit

Sometimes, pants hang too close to the ground and at uneven lengths. If you continue wearing pants this way, the edges may become frayed from too much friction with the ground. A quick fix solution is to fold the pants to the heel length. The fold may look very bulky and, over time, the new edge will also fray, damaging the fabric. The extra length can also cause the person to trip, which is dangerous.

Fabric Needs

You need to trim the garment below the thighline by decreasing the amount of fabric. If there are ruffles or pleats on the edge, you can adjust on the fabric itself or include the details in the shortening. If there are flares on the knee, the adjustment may be above or below the knee level.

Recommended Alteration Method: Pivot Method

1. Measure the leg length on both legs and mark the new hemline on the pants. You want to measure both legs as some clients may have asymmetrical legs.
2. Choose an appropriate pattern based on the client's measurements.
3. Mark the hems of both legs ½ inches from the original hemline to the new one in the front crease. Trim the allowance and see if the pattern now matches the measurements of the client.
4. To translate the pattern onto the fabric, place the pants on the table, mark it with ruler and chalk according to the pattern.
5. Cut the fabric carefully and stitch the hem in accurate measurements.
6. Press it evenly to create the correct crease.
7. Let the client try the clothes on and adjust any minor changes needed.

Chapter 12:
Project VII: Add Pockets to a Shirt

Adding pockets is both stylish and functional. Pocket detailing can add excitement to a bare area and contribute to the aesthetic appeal of the shirt. It is also very handy to put small items in pockets such as keys, money or cards. This dual purpose makes the skill of adding of pockets an important one for any tailor.

If you plan to put a pocket on your shirt, the shirt itself must fit your client well. There are male and female patterns for bodices and these shirts and dresses that must first have been created for you to add the design to. The pockets are just an additional detail and should not distract you from the basics of fitting a good shirt or dress.

Analyse the Body

Understand where the hands can go naturally in a shirt or dress. The usual positions are in the chest area or in the waist. Do not place pockets in areas which are unreachable to the hands or will make the wearer uncomfortable in any way.

Analyse the Fit

The appropriate location and size of the pockets is essential to the aesthetic and functional value of pockets. They should be placed in areas of easy access to the hands. The depth of the pocket must also be appropriate. You don't want a shallow pocket because that will limit its functional capacity. You also don't want a pocket that is too deep because that may look unflattering on a shirt or dress when you have too many things inside the fabric. There are standard sizes according to the fit of the bodice. You can customize your own depending on the measurements of the client, the aesthetic value you are targeting and the functional capacity the client needs.

Fabric Needs

Proper placement and size of the pockets is important. There are lots of pocket patterns available. It is advisable that the pattern in the shirt matches the pocket. They should not clash in terms of colors, textures or pattern. Otherwise, the pocket will stand out which is not the effect you want to go for. Choose an appropriate pocket pattern for the shirt or dress you will add it to.

Recommended Alteration Method

1. Choose the pocket pattern that is most appropriate for your purposes. There are commercial pocket patterns available or you can design your own. Experiment with the kinds of fabrics you have. Excess fabric may be transformed into a pocket if you're feeling creative.
2. Determine the final position of the pocket. For the chest area, choose either the left or right

chest area in between the scyeline and the center front. For waist pockets, place them near the hip.

3. Mark the placement of the pockets with pins. Ensure that the pockets are placed symmetrically. A 5 inch opening of the pocket is optimal so incorporate that to the design.
4. Cut out the pocket patterns on the fabric you will be using. Create stitching lines with allowances of ¼ inch.
5. Locate the side seams near the pocket area you have determined. Cut out the stitches on the side seams.
6. Stitch the pocket with a ¼ inch allowance from the edge.
7. Sew the side seams and then iron the side seams. Try the dress or shirt on and allow the client to place their hands on the pockets. The fit must be comfortable, with the opening not too wide and not too small.

Final Words

Congratulations! You should have completed your first projects. Now that you have made all seven sewing projects, you're almost ready to launch your own collection! I hope you didn't rush through as each activity was meant to be enjoyed. Hopefully, also, you were able to apply the standards of fitting and the selection of patterns to guide you in your sewing.

I would advise you to take a picture of your unfinished and finished sewing projects. Take a picture of the patterns you used and the final dress or shirt or skirt you have altered. This will be good for you to document your progress. When you look at the pictures, you can see objectively which parts you may have missed in altering well. You can zoom in on little seam showings or pockets not lying along the structural lines. This is not just about analyzing minute details; it serves as feedback to learn from and build on for your next projects. Don't be careless and think that the client will not spot those little errors. Sometimes, when we are so focused on sewing the tiny details on clothes, we tend to forget the bigger picture. When you take a picture of the finished project, you see how the different patterns come together to make a unified whole. Aim for excellence even if you make mistakes in each project. If you have this goal, then you will work hard to achieve it.

More importantly, I want you to take a picture with each person you have made those clothes for. Make them wear it in your shop. Let them try it on for you. Ultimately, sewing is not just a relationship with fabrics, it is a relationship with real people. Your goal is not to make perfect clothes that look good in a catalogue or in pictures. The goal of sewing is to make clothes for people that fit well and feel good.

This also serves as a reference or resource for you as you take on more and more projects. Document the progress of your alteration by using the pictures of people to help you remember a particular project. When you have a problem with adjusting the sleeves, think of Mrs. Brown who came to you with a lot of fabric hanging around her wrist. What did you do? How did you adjust the length? Instead of focusing on the measurements, you get to remember the person and then the recall becomes better and you have a template to work from. When you catalogue your work, you are actually making your own portfolio for other people to see just how good you are.

In the introduction, I told you about my peculiar way of asking about a client's main problem. Instead of asking, "What do you want me to do?" I asked my clients "What look do you want?" This simple rephrasing of the question launches conversations on body size and family stories, on dreams and aspirations. I would like to end with my own way of closing a project with clients. Some tailors would leave the finished project in sealed bags and let the customer pick it up and the payment seals the deal. If further alterations or tweaks to the existing alterations are needed, the customer can always go back and have it fixed in a jiffy. Contract ended. I find that too mechanical and rather abrupt, not to mention inefficient. With a transactional manner of dispensing projects, the lack of communication will make the clients unnecessarily come back and forth to get the fit right.

My technique is to invite the client to try the clothes in the shop. I prefer that the client take some time to try the clothes on where I could see them and I can make instant alterations. I give them space to change and let them put on the newly-altered clothes. The moment they walk out of the changing room, you know that you have made a good project based on the way the clients carry themselves. Invite them to look at themselves in a full-sized mirror. Allow them to take a look at how the clothes fit them, from one side to another. Let them move in the clothing, exploring positions which may cause tension, feeling how the clothes will fit when they are sitting or walking. Let them feel how a well-fitted set of clothes should feel like. Give them a moment with their new clothes. And then ask them finally, "How do you feel wearing this dress or shirt?" It is the reply to this question that will affirm your vocation as a tailor.

Some of the memorable replies were: "I feel very tall when I put this on" or "I feel very beautiful and elegant in this dress." I feel giddy inside when some people with poor posture suddenly try to match the clothes they are in by adopting a better stance. Others can't help starting at themselves at the mirror. I take that as a compliment any day. When people begin liking themselves in the clothes they wear, I feel that I have done a good job.

These subtle effects show us that clothes are not just fabrics that we put on to cover our bodies. Clothes should help reflect who people are inside. If you don't feel confident, put on a well-fitted shirt and pants and let that help you reach that confidence you need. If you feel you are too small, let a well-fitted set of trousers give you the extra height you need. Ultimately, as tailors, we are not just changing clothes; we are changing the people wearing those clothes.

When you end a project this way, there is a 100 percent assurance that the client will come back to you. When you touch them in a profound way, through the emotions, they appreciate it. They feel that their opinions are valued and that you aren't just there for the money. You begin establishing a relationship with your clients and word will spread very fast. They are going to recommend you to their families and friends, to their coworkers and superiors. Before long, your shop is going to compete very well with my business. Establish these relationships because you will be seeing these people for a very long time.

My final advice to you is to sew, sew, and sew. Keep making new projects because that is the only way you are going to learn. You will become better at cutting the length of trousers if you do it over and over again. One good trousers alteration is a lucky accident; making well-fitting trousers again and again is a sign of mastery. Once you get better at the basics, you might try your hand in intermediate difficulty projects which I will be teaching you in another book. Remember to keep sewing. You shouldn't let a day pass by when you don't trace a pattern, stitch a seam or simply handle fabrics. The hand has a way of remembering so you cannot be an occasional alterations tailor. Practice, practice, practice!

It is also a good exercise to observe people. When you are sitting in a park or riding on the subway, try looking at people and their clothes. Learn to spot good-fitting clothes and those that aren't. Observe what clothes are becoming trendy, and how people move with their clothes. In this way, you are extending your shop to the entire neighbourhood.

I hope you enjoyed this book and I look forward to meeting you in succeeding projects. I think tailors should learn from other tailors because we all share that passion for people and what they wear. Keep on sewing!